BASIC GUIDE TO MANICURES 101

Step by step techniques to your nails crafting

Jaylen Leila

Table of Contents

CHAPTER ONE

INTRODUCTION

Why do people get manicures? First, your self-esteem can be affected by changing your nails. Professional women who had lost their jobs felt guilty about having to forgo a weekly manicure. Second, it is a relaxing process, with the hands being massaged and each finger being carefully inspected. A third reason is that it can be hard to refuse a bride who has made manicures a requirement for her bridal party.

No matter the reason, a manicure requires you to be present for yourself. You can spend this time with your friend or chat with the manicurist. You and the manicurist are practically one another, and if you get to know each other well you may catch up on your lives since your last manicure.

Even if you don't get along well with your nail technician, you can still benefit from a manicure. Nail biters might be tempted to stop chewing on their nails if they see a manicure with Moon Over Mumbai polish.

Some people don't see the point in spending an hour at a nail salon. Manicures won't last forever. That's why salons can count on customers coming back for more. If you aren't careful with your hands, your manicure may chip in as little as three days. A manicure can last for a week on average. A clear top coat can be added every other day to extend the life of your manicure.

Even if you have never put a pinky nail in a salon, it is possible to be curious about the women and men in your life who go missing behind those glass doors every week. Continue reading to find out about manicures, and the secrets behind beautiful hands.

Contents

Canyon Coral, or Power Lunch?

- Polishing, Buffing, and Massaging, at Last
- Salon Manicure Safety
- Home Manicures

Fake Nails, or Real Nails Pink Parka, Canyon Coral, or Power Lunch?

Start with your choices. Ask a friend to recommend a salon. You can also check the Web site of your local health department to find a list if licensed or penalized salons.

Next, you need to decide between fake and real

nails. Fake nails are a good option if you don't like your nails. But how fake should it be? You can glue the tips of your nails with plastic artificial tips glue. Yo ur entire nail will be covered in full artificial nails . These can be made of plastic and glued to your nails. You can also have sculpted nails. In this technique, the technician creates a new nail using air-drying acrylic.

You can polish fake nails with gel which hardens into a gloss or acrylic which is made of a powder and is thicker. Fake nails can be more expensive (ranging from $20 to $100 depending on how long they stay), but they provide a larger canvas for the nail technician to work with. Nail biters can have trouble chewing through acrylic nails, even those that are beautiful.

Ask for natural nails if you prefer regular nail polish. This option is what we assume, and we will walk you through all the steps.

The manicurist will first direct you to a variety of polishes in hundreds of colors and then ask you to choose one. Do not assume that all salons offer cheap polish. They don't want to see you complaining about chipped nails. The longest step for the indecisive is choosing one polish from the neons, glitters, solids, sheers, and solids.

The manicurist and you will then go to a table where the real art begins. The manicurist will ask you to pick a nail shape. Round nails are popular, but you can avoid ingrown nails and hangnails by not filing the corners. Your manicurist will shape your nails with an emeryboard.

Then, you will receive a bowl of warm soapy water. Place your hand in the bowl, and allow it to soak. This cuticle softening and cleaning step kills bacteria and fungi so your nails aren't damaged or infected. A fan placed on the table will dry your nails after the finger bath.

Buffing, massaging, and polishing at Last

We now move on to the more difficult stuff for both first-timers as well as old-timers: cuticle work. The manicurist will first push your cuticles off of your nails. If you don't ask, your hangnails will then be trimmed using cuticle scissors.

Why can't we leave our cuticles alone? Manicurists believe that cuticles can grow too fast. You shouldn't paint the cuticle strip that covers your nails because it will chip quickly.

Next comes buffing. This smoothes out ridges and helps polish adhere.

The massage is the final step in relaxation. Different salons have their own signatures. You may feel your hands soak in the steam of a hot towel. The manicurist will then apply lotion to your hands and massage you up to the elbows.

These two steps will remove any barriers between your

nails, and the polish. To remove old paint and lotion, the manicurist will wipe your nails with alcohol. The manicurist will apply oil remover to your nails if they are oily. The color.

A clear base coat is applied to each nail. This prevents any colored polish from staining. A fan or UV lamp is used to dry your nails after each coat. Because of the risk of cancer, some salons use fans.

Next comes colored polish. Next, the manicurist

paints one of your fingers and asks you if you like this particular color. Give honest answers. It is easier to make a change right away than it is after you have applied the two required coats.

You don't need to limit your nail art choices to just color. There are many options. This includes charms, glitters, charms and decals as well as rhinestones and dried flowers. You can also airbrush other patterns like your initials. A manicurist can also paint designs by hand.

Your new handiwork is completed with a clear top coat. This final layer slows down chipping. Do not touch any nail polish at this stage. The manicurist will temporarily assume control of your hands and move you and your belongings to a drying table. Fans or a UV lamp will help set the polish. The manicurist will then apply a quick drying solution after five to ten minute. Once your nails are dry, you can now use your hands.

Do not touch the door. You will need to pay. However, you can also pay before the paint is applied. The price of a manicure will vary depending on where you are. It may cost $15 to $15, depending on whether the salon is fancy, if there are many salons nearby, and if you choose a manicure-pedicure combo. The manicurist should be tipped. Most salons will ask you to tip cash.

Men's manicures

Fact: Men get manicures. The process for men is the same as that for women: shaping, cuticle cleansing and then nail buffing. Some men prefer no polish while others want a matte or clear polish to make their nails shine. The manicure is the same for men and women, regardless of whether you use polish or not.

We asked a manicurist if she believed that manicures are most popular with men because they love to look good. She said that manicures are more popular with men than for women once they become addicted to them.

CHAPTER TWO

SALON MANICURE SAFETY

The salon was not there to do a manicure or cure fungus. You can be careful and the only thing that will bloom on your fingers is fake flowers.

Look for licenses, which are the official stamps that confirm legality and cleanliness. The state health department must approve any salon that is located in the United States. The state health department ensures that all metal tools are sterilized, and that any other tools are disposed of or cleaned between customers. The state board of cosmetology must also be certified as a nail technician. The state board of cosmetology requires that the nail technician has completed 600 hours of supervision and courses in order to be licensed.

This license means that the salon can perform manicures cleanly. However, they don't guarantee that the salon will perform the manicure correctly on the day you visit. Warts and nail fungus are the most common infections at nail salons. The problem starts with the person who is infected. Salons don't sterilize instruments properly, which can lead to more problems. The manicurist may then use your instruments to spread viruses or fungi. To get infected, you still need to have breaks in your skin. This can be caused by ripping your cuticles. You can make the breaks by buffing your cuticles or clipping them during manicure.

Avoiding cuticle pushing or clipping will protect you from salon infections. Dr. Kent Aftergut, a dermatologist from the University of Texas Southwestern Medical Center in Dallas, says that people often let manicurists damage their cuticles. I know that some people don’t like how their cuticles look. Cuticles are best left alone from a medical standpoint. Aftergut says that cuticles are what distinguish your nail bed from all the rest of the world, including bacteria, fungi, and viruses.

Aftergut says that the best protection is to have your own equipment. It can be purchased for as low as $60. It is a common sight in salons, and many don't mind it at all. They will even store your instruments in a bag for you. This way you don't need to depend on the salon to sterilize properly.

Pedicure peril

You might like to do manicure-pedicure combinations, so be aware of "whirlpool footbaths." Although they are rare, whirlpool feetbaths can inflict serious infections with the atypical *mycobacteria*. These microbes can infect any cut or nick on your skin. You may get boils, rounds and antibiotics, as well as scarring on your legs, if you are infected.

The design of the whirlpool footbath poses a risk. It absorbs municipal water which is contaminated with the microbe. The water leaves the bath and travels through a screen. Microbes thrive on this screen. However, the majority of these baths were removed by the health department.

"Trust your salon that they don't use footbaths that circulate the water through pipes." advises Aftergut.

Home Manicures

You can also stay at home and do your nails yourself in your pajamas. All you need is the right equipment, and enough time. You will need an emeryboard and nail clippers to shape your nails. You will need to remove old polish using cotton balls and polish remover. You will need a buffer to smoothen the nails if you desire it.

You don't need to use cuticle products, but it is a good idea to consult a dermatologist before you start trimming your cuticles. A cuticle softener is required if you insist on trimming. You can save money by switching to professional cuticle oil. To push the cuticle off of the nail, you'll need a cuticle stick made from wood and cuticle scissors. You'll also need a base coat and colored polish, as well as a top coat.

Keep your scissors and clippers clean and dispose of any disposables after use to avoid infection. Do not share your supplies with your spouse, friend, or significant other.

You'll pay less for this equipment if you purchase generic brands, and more than $150 if you choose professional-grade products.

www.ingramcontent.com/pod-product-compliance
Ingram Content Group UK Ltd.
Pitfield, Milton Keynes, MK11 3LW, UK
UKHW021931200726
13853UKWH00010B/30

9 798758 444689